9 Quantum SECRETS Of ABUNDANCE

Attracting the Life You Want

Warren Atiba Taylor

9 Quantum Secrets of Abundance

By Warren Atiba Taylor

2014

9 Quantum Secrets of Abundance

TABLE OF CONTENTS

INTRODUCTION

This book is about my journey, it is about a quest for answers that have encompassed my entire life, even when I was a little boy of about 5 or 6 years old attending a little country Methodist Presbyterian Church in Richmond, Va. This book is about you, for we are all connected; in the new global information age we are as close as a few keystrokes and an internet signal.

How This Book Came Into Being

Before leaving to move to Brazil in October of 2013, I was hopeful, excited, and scared. Although I had been mildly successful as a musician, a parent, and as a composer, I was enthused about the trip. I was leaving the USA, because of the total implosion and indifference of the music business in the American (at least in my reality), and to give it a final try in Brazil as I hadn't really succeeded as an artist in the Ole US of A.

So after over 35 years of studying Christianity, Islam, Tibetan Buddhism, metaphysics, and finally quantum physics, I still felt I hadn't achieved what I'd desired. I'd recently lost my gorgeous Brazilian girlfriend to another guy, partly for not getting back to Brazil soon enough on my original journey. My 21 year old daughter was upset because I was leaving, yet acted like everything was okay, until I left. My mother thought I was crazy for leaving my still in college daughter, and leaving the comfort and safety of Richmond, Va. At 56 years old, still trying to live the Artist's dream.

Not being a big prayer guy, I had only one request before leaving the States and it was as follows:

"Dear Universe / God / I Am Presence or Whatever Presence Exists!, "Will you please tell me, show me or direct me to whatever principles I don't know, but need to know to be

be successful and acquire the things in life I want?" This book is a short version of the principles I began to acquire that have been life changing.

I was directed by synchronicity and personal research to read books on physics, Einstein's Theory of Relativity, Quantum Physics and other books that were beginning to bridge the gap between **metaphysics** and **physics**. I will refer to these books from time to time, and I will list a group of books that you can use to further your study in the bibliography.

I believe that we live our lives using the Principles of the Law of Attraction, Quantum Physics, and Vibrational Theory knowingly or unknowingly. I submit that IF we can find a blueprint to effectively change our Emotion and Thought processes by changing our beliefs in a positive way, then we can create and attract what we want. I offer you one such formula that is working in amazing ways for me.

Some of these ideas will be new, some of them you already know, and others will challenge your way of thinking and emoting. I only ask that you allow yourself to stay open to the possibility of creating the life you want, through initiating huge positive shifts in your consciousness and that will show up as life changing shifts of Infinite Abundance in your reality.

Enjoy!

CHAPTER I

V
Vibration, Who and What We Are

You are a vibrational being,
You are a transmitter.
You are a receiver.

You are your thoughts and you are more than your thoughts, for you create and shape your reality through the manipulation of matter as thought and emotion. Your ability to create the life you want is influenced by your beliefs and by your ability to understand your emotions as indicators of how much control you have of your life. When Max Planck first discovered the quantum, the smallest measurable part of matter, he not only changed the face of physics, but he changed the future of humanity.

For by observing the smallest element of change in our emotions, not only do we become observers, we become aware that we are creators of our reality, knowingly or unknowingly.

Today physicists and meta-physicists are meeting as equals and realizing that not only are you an observer of reality, we are creators, because it has been proven that in many physics experiments that the observer affects the results. So in essence we create by our ability to observe and to manipulate our emotion through thought, particularly meditation and contemplation. Emotion = energy in motion.

What if you could change how you feel by simply changing your thinking and possibly your beliefs? An additional strategy would require tuning into an emotional frequency that is more conducive to your attracting what you want?

They is no time in the universe that matter is not occurring change. This theory is called the Quantum of Change. So why does this matter? Because matter, like thought is always changing, only we cannot perceive it with our 5 senses. But as we become better observers, our emotions then become quantum indicators of our thinking and thus we can affect change by changing how we feel.

First in order to create change, we must understand the brain.

The reptilian brain came into being in man hundreds of thousands of years ago as a means of continued existence. It makes decisions based solely on survival, friend/foe, food/not food, and it makes this decision in seconds or less. It does not examine consequences.

The Paleomammalian brain came later, it is like the mammal's brain, it does consider consequences but its decisions based on emotion.

The Neomammilian brain is a human adaption and it uses logic to make decisions.

This is the part of the brain that separates us from animals.

However the Paleomammalian brain makes decisions based on emotion. Much of the programming of the mammalian part of our brain is subconscious.

There is a part of our subconscious brain that makes decisions based on the input of our emotions. It is called the reticular activation system, which I will refer to as the RAS. The RAS is like a huge filtering center, kind of like a computerized post office, but much more sophisticated. To a great extent your ability to facilitate change, is directly tied to subconscious beliefs you have about yourself. The RAS accesses your beliefs and through this system many of your decisions are made in tenths of seconds by this great innovation of nature.

Your subconscious beliefs are a product of beliefs you accepted from your parents, school, peers and society. Many of these beliefs are false or don't work toward you creating the highest expression of yourself. Much of humanity would rather be right than know the truth. So in order to attract what you want you are going to have to examine many of the beliefs that you hold dear.

In order to create abundance you need a formula that allows you to raise your emotional feelings about yourself and get more in touch with emotional indicators that are the rudder to how you are managing and creating your life.

Your emotions are tied to neural connections in your brain and in order to change how you feel, you must create new neural connections. These new neural connections will affect your decision making process. As you become more open to the infinite nature of your consciousness, you will begin to attract more of what you want and less of what you don't want.

You have received programming from your parents, your education, your religious or spiritual beliefs, your peers and especially the media. Without a new paradigm that allows you to freely choose your emotional state; you are more a reactionary being than a being free to be the powerful creator of worlds that you can be.

The first step to attracting the things you want is learning how to change your emotions consciously and subconsciously and to understand "Who You Are."

CHAPTER 2

I
Imagery and Imagination

You are a creature of great imagination and power. Your brain, ears, eyes, nose and sense of touch make calculations in thousandths of a second. You are connected to God or as I prefer the Universal Presence by your consciousness. Colors, sounds and pictures are inputted to your brain and become symbols and the symbols represent ideas, and you give these ideas meaning and structure.

You attract what you want based on your unconscious beliefs and you validate what you believe about the world through your experience. Because much of humanity has been programmed to think that outside forces have more control over our life than we do as individuals, then this brainwashing becomes a self fulfilling prophecy for billions of people.

However, you can change your life by examining daily what beliefs and emotions may be sabotaging your life, accepting the unlimited nature of your consciousness, and imagining the INFINITE POSSIBILITIES that exist in your experience.

The Request
Ask
Answer – The Universe Answers
Allow – you allow the reality of your experience to receive your request.

This is the simple formula for creating your abundance. I learned this valuable formula in the book Ask and It Is Given, by Esther and Jerry Hicks.

What can you imagine? What imagery moves your emotions? What words and synonyms can you use to facilitate the emotion of peace, acceptance, interest, enthusiasm, devotion, confidence, inspiration and love.

How You Relate

The way and manner that you relate to friends, family and business associates is a learned behavior. Your happiness or sadness can be directly traced to how authentic, how honest and how self expressive you are at any moment.

The natural exuberance, joy, intelligence and cooperativeness that is the highest expression of you can only shine forth when you do not allow past failures and mistakes to control how you feel about yourself at present. These past failures, mistakes and bad relationships are stored experiences that influence your life consciously and unconsciously.

In order to change this pattern of thinking, first you have to remember the unlimited nature of your consciousness. Then you can start the programming the positive ideas that will elicit you feeling good about yourself regardless of how many failures you've had in the past.

Remember you are your thoughts but you are also more than your thoughts

Each memory is attached to an emotion and strong memories have an electrical charge associated with them. You experience these past memories charged with electricity as an emotion.

The secret is to create new images, new neural pathways of success. Initially you will create the new neural pathways by imagining, and moving up the Emotional Reference chart (see Appendix A).

As you tune into emotions higher up on the emotional reference chart... i.e. confidence, enthusiasm, elation, excitement, joy and love; then when you make your requests you will be in a STATE OF FEELING GOOD. For otherwise you will only sabotage your request because of your resistance, which could be an effect of doubt, fear, low self value, frustration, depression and many other negative emotions. In order to implement this new formula you will need to suspend your previous way of being, long enough to create the new beliefs and emotions that will begin to reflect your outer reality. "As above so below".

By creating this state of Feeling Good, this highest expression of you, you will begin to expect your requests to be answered, and because you are broadcasting from a higher state of awareness you allow the source to provide you what is rightfully yours. In essence you are actually manifesting what already exists!!

CHAPTER 3

B
The Best You

The best you is happy, the best you is enthusiastic and cooperative, the best you is loving, the best you has all of its financial needs met, with enough to spare and to share.

In order to continually communicate the highest expression of yourself, in order to get to the highest expression of yourself, you must continually get present to your lower emotions and be ready and able to transform them into the love, joy, and confidence that is closer to your highest vibration.

In essence your daily practice will be guarding and keeping your mind as peaceful, loving, supportive and joyful of yourself as you possibly can.

As you invoke this new way of being, you will see and attract more and more opportunities that will confirm that you are creating the highest expression of yourself.

Your daily practice will also include your also requesting the source to make you aware of what hidden and self sabotaging belief systems you need to change to be the Best you.

After consistently using this formula for some time, it will become your way of being, you will handle negative emotions quickly as the indicators they are, and you will be constantly searching for new and wonderful ways of expressing the Best You.

How is this achieved? This state of feeling good can be achieved by the practice of meditation, contemplation and prayer. As you start to feel better about yourself, you start to attract more of what you want, which reinforces the realization that you are a broadcaster and receiver of energy. When you are feeling good, you are broadcasting and receiving good positive energy.

Abundance, love, excitement, enthusiasm, confidence, devotion.

When you are feeling bad, you are attracting and broadcasting negative energy; depression, despair, anger, disappointment, worthlessness, guilt etc

However, much to our dismay often we need these lower vibrating emotions as true indicators of what we presently feel, as indicators of our relationship to our reality. Otherwise we keep repeating the same mistakes in the process of learning how to express ourselves clearly, confidently and with power. You need to be able to express pain, anger, disappointment, frustration, anxiety and depression without suppression.

For until you can express the entire range of emotions, until you get present to your lower emotions in a healthy and transformative way, it is difficult to authentically move up the emotional scale. For if we skip over the unpleasant side of ourselves in this process, we suppress what is really happening with our emotional self. The good news is that in this process you get to choose how long you will stay in a particular emotion with the Emotional Reference Chart exercise.

Remember all emotions are indicators, and these indicators were given to us by the source as a means to sense the need for change and to be authentically present to our environment.

How do we change our emotions?

We change our emotions by meditation, contemplation and "Being Present".

I provide a great technique for changing your emotional self in the Emotional Reference Chart Exercise in Appendix A. This is an exercise where you get to practice "getting present" to your emotional state and then transforming your emotional state as you move up the chart.

Just as we are more than our thoughts, we are more than our emotions. The practice of meditation allows us to be non-attached to our emotional state so that we can be receptive to change. Realizing the fluidity of our emotional self provides us with the opportunity to control our emotional self. This also allows us to have a greater choice in our emotional range and not be so reactionary emotionally when life doesn't go our way.

What an incredible freedom and power!

As you start to feel better about yourself, you will begin to notice how the universal source is frequently sending you information on how to improve your life. As you develop a greater relationship with the highest expression of yourself you become intuitive in your decision making.

As you become more comfortable with the idea of accessing the quantum field of energy through this transformational emotional process, you create even more positive momentum and strengthen your connection to the source of all things.

CHAPTER 4

R
Resistance

You are a part of the source of All That Is and because you are a vibratory being in a Quantum Field of Infinite Possibilities or QFP, you attract what you broadcast, even though you may not realize it. But because of the nature of manifestation, there is a time delay that allows you to be selective in what you manifest.

Why does it take so long?

That time delay in attracting your good is there to allow you the clarity to make wise choices about what you are attracting.

Your resistance takes the form in many facets; it shows up as fear, failure, and procrastination. All of the aforementioned emotions or feelings are various forms of self sabotage. They manifest in your reality as the manifestation of things that you do not want.

In every decision, in every moment of creation there are at least two actions of creation that are occurring for you. You are either attracting the thing you want, or if you are resisting your natural good, you are attracting the thing that you do not want.

At the end of this book I have created an appendix that will give you exercises to overcome your resistance to your good. (Appendix B is a simple formula similar to what scientists use in creating and testing hypotheses.) With this formula/template you will begin the scientific process of attracting what you want by simply "Asking".

Why do I use the term hypothesis? Well Webster defines a hypothesis as a tentative assumption made to draw out and test its logical consequence.

Accepting the idea that you can change and attract what you want by reprogramming your subconscious beliefs will take time and effort.

At first you will need to prove that this formula works, and that's why I used the term hypothesis. If you stay open to the possibility; you will be amazed at how well the system can work. You will need to trust in this new definition of who you are and what you can do. There will be times when you will need to examine what is the source of your resistance. You will need to investigate what faulty hidden beliefs and feelings reside in your conscious and subconscious thinking that keep you from attracting what you want.

The source of all things is ever and always available to you. You must know and realize that you are never separate from this Source. Some call it God, All That Is, The Universe, Jehovah, Allah, the Buddha, Shiva, it has many names. Personally I like the Quantum Field of Infinite Possibilities or the Universal Presence.

GUILT, SELF CONDEMNATION AND LOW SELF VALUE

The Universe does not hold you guilty for your mistakes, it is not jealous, or limiting in anyway, man does a real great job of that, better than God or the Universal Presence could ever do in my opinion.

However, if you try to expand too fast this Universal Presence which is also a principle will force you to contract as a means of self preservation. Although you could do a 180 and go from being frustrated and angry to a state of Love/Elation immediately, usually it's a process that will happen step by step over a period of days or weeks.

In general this source is always expanding, in essence it is love. Much of your resistance is based on a belief that you are not good enough, not intelligent enough or not talented enough.

In handling resistance personally, I often remind myself that I am a part of this great Universal Presence. Quite often I just contemplate the Infinite Power and Love of the Great Universal Source and this begins to remove any resistance I have. Through the process of remembering you reaffirm your true nature.

By remembering your true nature then you will see the error of any belief that seems to deny you the power and truth of overcoming any problem.

Ironically, The Universal Power is always sending back to you what you broadcast consciously or unconsciously, which means a great many of us end up attracting the things we don't want because we are using this universal principle in reverse or without conscious knowledge.

CHAPTER 5

A
All That Is

The source of your good is All That Is. It is the life force that exists in all living matter; it is the attractive, electromagnetic force that holds together all matter.

Just as you have your physical senses of taste, touch, seeing, hearing, you have a psychological sense: emotion. Just like you have a rational self, you have an emotional self that operates on the conscious and subconscious planes.

The success in your life or lack of success is tied to the energy that drives your beliefs, for they are what drive you to accomplish what you want and to attract what is your life. The law of attraction which is directed by your beliefs and fueled by your emotions works in reverse just as easily as it works to move your life toward what you want.

When you intrinsically accept the idea that outside forces do not in actuality have more control of your life than you do, then this belief will be the dominant factor in determining your good or lack thereof. The law of attraction is not a new idea, but the idea that you can change your reality by changing your underlying beliefs about what you perceive is groundbreaking.

When we as individuals begin to believe this fundamentally, then we can begin to create a society where the great majority have more than enough abundance to share and to spare. Any belief that gives greater power to forces outside of your self places resistance between the self and the source of all things.

Once you begin to change or shift your beliefs about who you are, which is a vibrating conscious being surrounded by a Quantum Field of Infinite Possibilities, then you will begin to attract your unlimited good.

As you raise your emotional mood, you align yourself with the Source, and you energize the Quantum Field of Infinite Possibilities. The result of this change in belief will also draw to you the ideas, information, resources and people that will open up a doorway for you to become a clear receptor of unlimited abundance, joy, love, confidence, enthusiasm, and support.

Thoughts held in mind, beget their own kind.

CHAPTER 6

T
Test

Your life is a test of your ideas and your beliefs. It is as if the Source of All That Is has given you this incarnation to field test your ability to create your world.

Think for a moment... the universe is filled with infinite possibilities and you are one of those infinite possibilities. Physicists have proven that each of us is surrounded by a field of electromagnetic energy.

Some metaphysicists call this the aura; some people even have the ability to read your aura based on the color emitted by your emotions.

Let us examine a bit more what we are. Each of us exists as and within an electromagnetic field I will call the Quantum Field of Infinite Possibilities, or the QFIP. We make rational and emotional decisions based on the input we receive. Many of these decisions are made by the subconscious programming we have received as a part of the social and educational process. If we are to move to a new era in which the principles of quantum physics and metaphysics are as easy for our children as they are for physicists and mystics, we will have created a world consciousness that can usher in a new era of abundance for the majority and not the few.

Because our consciousness connects us to all things, an effect of this connection is that the power of our conscious awareness is magnified by our thoughts and emotions. The magnification occurs whether we are aware of it or not. You can see examples of this occurring in places throughout the world where we see small groups of people grow through the power of "social networks" that facilitate a change in thought and belief. This change in thought and belief creates a momentum of change that starts a domino effect that can change an entire society.

What if we could change not only our own field of possibilities by changing our thoughts and emotions? But in addition we could change our reality by simply asking for what we want, having a feeling of expectation about whatever we have asked for and observing what would occur. We are not only limited to receiving physical gifts, but the Source always has the information we need available to us as well.

INFORMATION REQUEST EXERCISE 1

Try this simple experiment to show that this Field of Possibilities works for you.

Ask the Source for a surprise to show me that you exist.

> **Dear Source,**
>
> **I would like a surprise, something good and unexpected, please give me a sign within 48 hours that you exist.**
> **Thank you**
> **Within ten days I found an apartment like this at almost the exact price I asked for.**

EXERCISE 2 INFORMATION REQUEST

Let's say that you are resisting letting go of some unhappy feeling. After getting dumped by my girlfriend, after 4 months, I still hadn't let go. So I wrote:

Dear Source, I would like to accept that my girlfriend just does not love me anymore and I must let go.

Please give me a sign that I am over her, that she will come back or that I better continue letting go. I would like this sign in 7 days

Thank you.

I remember the very next day, feeling awful and depressed about the situation. As I was riding my bike to a friend's I got caught in a terrible rainstorm. This meant for me that I had to wash my hands of this relationship, even though I may not have wanted to accept it. Sometimes in order to move forward in the process we have to let go of previously conceived ideas and feelings. This is a principle of the quantum of change.

For as in my example regret, guilt and despondency became acceptance. As in the principle of conservation of energy, no energy is ever lost it is just transformed.

CHAPTER 7

I

Insights and Intention

The loving energy that is All That Is, is ever communicating with you.

All the answers you need to attract what you want, to answer any question are available within you. You just need to ask.

Dear Source,   September 29, 10:07

Please show me whatever principles or ideas that I need to understand in order to be successful in my life.

This is the request I made before deciding to leave the US and live in Brazil again. Upon arriving, I got a notion to research the relationship between physics and metaphysics. Quantum theory is the study of the smallest measurement of observable matter, the quantum. Metaphysics is the study of the underlying spiritual principles that connect all spiritual paths. Meta = below, Physics – the science of matter.

In my research I begin to find books written by other authors that combine metaphysical principles and physics principles I explore in this book. During the process of changing my vibration by changing my emotions by changing my beliefs, I started to receive messages intuitively from the Universal Presence that I wrote about in this book. As you start to practice the exercises in this book, you will start to observe how your emotions influence your thoughts and how your thoughts influence your emotions.

So in essence when you cannot change your emotions quickly,

which I think will come with practice, you will notice how quickly you can change your thinking by deeply reflecting on a positive emotion, which in turn will change your emotional state. With practice you will acquire the ability to change your emotional vibration quickly and effectively, regardless of the challenges presented to you.

Exercise 3 Setting Your Emotional Intent

The purpose of this exercise is to get you to feel an emotion that might be higher on the emotional chart than your present emotional state. The emotional intent exercise allows you to increase your focus for a segment of time during your day, to experience the higher emotion and use that energy productively.

Whatever positive emotion you would like to experience: write it down on a sheet of paper. (You can use the Emotional Reference Chart if you like) Let's say you choose the word:

Hopeful/Optimism,

Using a dictionary of synonyms look up synonyms that apply to Optimism.... For example: confidence, buoyant, cheerfulness etc. Then write down statements using the synonyms you have come up with. As you do this exercise you will probably have one of two experiences. If you are feeling pessimistic then you will put up resistance to doing the exercise. That's okay. The way to overcoming resistance is to get present to your resistance. (See the last chapter on noticing for how to handle resistance better.)

Your positive journaling might look like this:

. I am optimistic because I have the tools I need to win
I am confident and prepared
I choose to be cheerful because I can resolve my problems better by being cheerful etc.

<u>If you have some resistance then your exercise might look like this:</u>

I am pessimistic because I can't seem to do anything right
I am cynical because things don't usually work out for me
I feel unenthusiastic because things are not going well.

I often use the "Intention Exercise" to strengthen parts of my workday efficiency and to examine emotional feelings that strengthen my connection to the source. One of the greatest lessons I have learned from this process is having learned to deeply love myself, being at peace with myself, accepting being alone and content. As you become more in tune with the higher emotional frequencies, you will begin to take on levels of joy, peace and tranquility that may surprise you.

The process of reprogramming our belief systems and becoming quantum observers is not one in which we ignore and suppress negative emotions or experiences.

Partnering

It would be very beneficial for you to get a partner that you can trust with your deepest and darkest emotions, who can provide honest

and supportive feedback during the process.

Partnership could be like having your own organic mirror to reflect what you will feel during this process. It's not about suppressing the emotion or as Greg Kuhn says "putting a happy face on it." It's about getting present, taking little steps up the emotional scale. Getting to a consistent state of deep self love, joy, passion, will require little steps, because the mind will put up resistance. The programming most of us have involves deep seated beliefs that are not in alignment with the highest expression of who we are... powerful, highly intelligent, loving beings surrounded by a Quantum Field of Infinite Possibilities.

Moreover, these principles provide a formula in which you can move up to the Feel Good State of a sense of Powerful Self Love by acknowledging areas that need realignment and then slowly (sometimes quickly) moving up the Emotional Reference Chart.

MORE ON INSIGHT

I love looking into dictionaries for synonyms of words I am researching. Insight is one I looked up in the writing of this book. The word intuition is associated with the word Insight. Now the Oxford Dictionary defines intuition as the ability to understand something immediately.

Buddhism has a type of insight that is called direct knowing which, in essence; means that we don't always have to go through a rational thought process to immediately have access to the answers we need. Through the power of your mind, the development of your emotional awareness, you will begin to know directly through the source all the answers to attract what you want and resolve the problems in your life.

Intuition; **synonyms** (n) feeling, hunch, insight, instinct, notion, premonition, presentiment, sense, suspicion, vision, **4.** ingenuity; **synonyms** (n) adroitness, cunning, ingeniousness, imagination, acumen, creativity

CHAPTER 8

O
Optimism and Openness to Change

One of the requirements of this new way of being, this new way of creating and attracting what you want is to develop a sense of optimism and openness to change. Start expecting your life to get better. Go to sleep expecting something good to occur tomorrow.

My examination of the quantum principles as a thought process goes something like this... I believe that the smallest amount of change in my thought process can produce the greatest effect.

By changing my thoughts, I change my beliefs about something. As I gain more confidence in my ability to create the life I want; wonderful opportunities show up in my life even faster. Recently, before traveling back to the US, I had this desire to perform at carnival in Brazil. After 3 years of living in Brazil, I had played a few festivals during the period, but I had never participated in a performance where I actually played the regional music during carnival.

I had made a request for extra money for my impending trip.
One evening as I was leaving the beach after a leisurely stroll I bumped into someone I had just met at an outdoor cultural event. Pedro is an event coordinator and event producer. He invited me to join one of his clients for two shows on consecutive days playing carnival music.

When you change your emotions to more positive ones you strengthen your will and your motive for being. When you realize that it is natural and easy to align yourself with the Universal Source that is All That Is; you raise the vibration that is you.

Then you quickly start to attract what you want not what you don't want

Changing your thinking > changes your beliefs > changes your emotion to more positive ones > aligns you with the Source.

I notice that whenever I have a need, quite often I first have to remind myself that I Am a part of the Great Source, the Universal energy, that is All That Is.

The only limitations on what I can receive are those I make up.

Simply by accepting this or being reminded of my true unlimited nature, I raise my energy. Then I can allow my good to come in, I can make any request and accept that it is done.

CHAPTER 9

N
Noticing

This book in a nutshell is about the Law of Attraction and how we can use this law to attract what we want using metaphysics and quantum principles.

To change your emotion will require work, for many people reading this book it may not be possible to go overnight from the lower emotional frequencies of depression, despair, anger, frustration, and doubt, to the higher vibrational frequencies of optimism, enthusiasm, excitement, passion to joyful/elated. It will require a process, a journey. In this last chapter I share a practice I was taught by my coach and friend Raven Dana.

It is a therapeutic practice calls Noticing.

What is Noticing?

> Well Oxford Dictionary defines the word notice as the announcement or warning of something.

I augmented the Oxford definition with a gestalt reference.

"Noticing is the process of paying attention to a change in thought and feeling which can be accompanied by sensations in the body, for example tightness in the shoulders, fluttering in the stomach, stress in any part of the body."

So noticing could be defined as being present to whatever feelings or sensations that are occurring mentally but are also are occurring physically in your present context.

In getting present with the emotions and feelings on the emotional chart in Appendix A, you will want to notice and then write down all of the negative emotions associated with a particular lower emotion, despair, worthlessness, grief etc.

For example:

I don't value my work
I am not intelligent enough.
I don't have enough education
I am too old.
I am ugly
I am overweight

All of your negative thoughts are a part of your reality at present, but they are not the best you, they are not the highest expression of yourself. The you that is at peace, the you that FEELS Good, that you that loves who you are and is content with who you are.

Ironically, the feeling of discontent is the desire that may have led you on your quest for truth.This feeling of discontent has led you on your quest to entertain the ideas in this book. So in the context of noticing; discontent is an emotional indicator of some desire for change. This message of change can also be a prompt or a cursor pointing you to seek to become more in alignment with the source of all things.

In order to do that you must look at your core beliefs about how you feel about yourself moment to moment. In order to realign yourself with the source you must raise your vibratory frequency or your emotional feeling. Then a doorway will open and you will consciously connect to the Quantum Field of Infinite Possibilities.

"Thoughts held in mind beget their own kind."

Why practice Noticing?

Remember practicing noticing is a therapeutic way to get present with what sensations the body is giving us. There are many medical studies that are beginning to show the relationship between physical health and emotional well being.

The body never lies. In actuality any type of body language can be an indicator for noticing. As you move up the emotional scale step by step, you will begin to gain confidence slowly at first that you have the ability to create the BEST YOU by "contemplating" more positive thoughts and realizing that you are trying on a new way of being, that the "Opportunity for Change" exists.

The Quantum of Change

Imagine for a moment that you, your life, emotions, struggles, accomplishments, beliefs, thoughts and your feelings are all composed of various combinations of the smallest elements in matter physicists call the quantum. Now contemplate that within your body is enough quantum energy to power a major city or destroy one.

Your consciousness is the observer and the creator of the motion of these elements. Consequently your desires, your will, your thoughts and your beliefs are the fuel drives the electrical, magnetic energy that attract and manifest your reality through your emotions.

Your conscious awareness is also the road map, and your unconscious awareness is the underlying program that is directing all the various parts of this quantum you. In this book I have provided a set of principles that can facilitate tremendous positive change in your life. Experiment, amplify, test and most of all enjoy the process of manifesting the highest expression of you.

Joy, Love, Prosperity and Abundance

Whatever you need is available

Ask

Give thanks

Allow

Answer

Appendix A

THE EMOTIONAL REFERENCE CHART

The emotional reference chart is a resource for examining your emotional tone, examining what you need to work on. In this way you can discern what is blocking you from your highest good.

I have created an exercise similar to one I found in Jerry Hick's Book, Ask and It is Given. I added a few of my own personal twists. Any emotion state that you are in at present is an indicator of the strength of your connection to the source. If you experiencing a sense of loss, depression, sadness or any emotion lower on the chart you can change your emotional level by tuning into an emotion higher on the chart. But don't skip over the emotional level where you are.

For example, let's say that you are feeling depressed about your job prospects; you have put in applications, you have done the background research and you have some possibilities. Find an emotion on the chart that corresponds to anticipation or expectation. Sit and contemplate the idea that you are anticipating a good result. You are expecting something good to occur tomorrow.

As an exercise it might look like this.

I anticipate that I will eventually get a job I live.

I have value and I expect a positive change in my life toward work.

Tomorrow I expect and anticipate some positive sign that I will find work.

Today, I feel better because I have a positive expectation and I realize the power of change.

Remember the Theory of the Quantum of Change. There is no time in reality that is without change. Whatever you focus on, wherever your **attention** is, that's where you emotional will go. As you start to contemplate a higher more positive emotion, you will see that you breathing, you thoughts and then your emotions will start to slowly and sometimes very quickly embrace this new state. Sometimes you will have to stay with a new emotional feeling for several days. Experiment!

I often try to stay in an emotion higher up the chart 1-3 days. I know that there will be days that are more challenging. Those are the days that I must do more work in contemplation (10.) I must move up the scale and I like to choose expectation. Because then I begin to simply accept the idea that I will feel better.

   Step 1 Choose an emotion on the reference chart

   Step 2 Write down your feelings about why you feel that emotion at present

   Step 3 Stay with the emotion for 1-3 days

   Step 4 Move up the emotion chart one step, repeat step 1 -3

1. Love, devotion, peacefulness, empowerment
2. Satisfaction, fulfillment
3. Happiness, power, self control
4. Radiant
5. Excitement, Enthusiasm
6. Positive Anticipation, Expectation
7. Optimism, Eagerness

8. Hopeful, Cheerful
9. Attentiveness, Curiosity
10. Calm, content, acceptance
11. Meditative, Contemplative
12. Sad, Cheerless
13. Apathy, Indifference
14. Unease, Discontent
15. Disappointment, Impatient, frustration
16. Exhaustion, apprehension
17. internalized Anger/Defeat
18. Vengeance, Condemnation
19. Anxiety, rage
20. Envy, Resentment
21. Insecurity, Unworthiness
22. Resignation, Hopelessness, Depression

Appendix B

THE REQUEST

In chapter 1, I talked about the idea that we are vibrating beings, receivers and transmitters in a field of electromagnetic energy. If we accept this premise as true, then not only are you transmitting energy, through your thoughts, words and physical activity, your are receiving energy though thought, word and physical activity. This next exercise is what I call "the Request." I have covered this exercise earlier but I give more background on how the Request works here.

The Request is a hypothesis, a question, a need, and in some ways it is a test. You always receive an answer, although you don't always receive the answer you expect.

Although in essence this exercise is a request, it is also a hypothesis because at first you will need to prove to yourself that this type of principle can work in your life. As a question, it is an opportunity for you find out information that you need.

As a need, it could be simply asking for a pay increase, a job, or a healing. Finally, it is also a test experience and experiment. As a test experience you will find that quite often you request is granted, however it there is any resistance, if there is a feeling behind your request that....

"I am not good enough"

I don't really believe in this hocus pocus.

So after writing in this fashion although the request would normally be granted, your resistance won't allow the request to be answered in a timely fashion.

If this happens then it would be a good idea to go back and check your beliefs about what happened or did not happen in the context of your request.

Here's a common request I make as a freelance musician:

THE REQUEST

Dear QFP/Universal Presence   (Time/Date)

This month I need XYZ dollars for rent, food etc. (need, desire, information).

Please send me enough work, shows, to cover my expenses, additionally I would like to have an extra $xxxx.xx after my bills are covered.

Please give me a sign in 48 hours that this request is being honored.

Thank You.

Okay , let's take a look at the template.

Address and Time Date : Dear FP/ Universal Presence Jan 1, 2014

Request: Please send ......

Ask for a sign: the sign can be of any time, I like to keep my requests short. For long term requests you can experiment. But on average I keep the request for a sign or indication to no more than a week.

Show of Gratitude: Thank You

Appendix C

FINDING YOUR NEW VOCATION THROUGH YOUR HEART'S DESIRE

In this new digital age, the new currency is the currency of ideas. With the mass laying off of millions of workers, the New Economy has sent a message to the world "retool, re-educate or else."

In this exercise you will use the Quantum Field and a little bit of meditation to find your heart's desire. Some of you may have already found your heart's desire, but may be struggling with no "the what" but the "how". Can I do it successfully enough to make a living? Can I even attract the money I need doing it?

THE FIRST STEP

1. ASK

If you are searching for an answer as to where to start; then you question might look like this.

Dear QFIP/God/Universe,

I need to know what is my life's vocation and I need clear direction as to where to begin. If you already know your vocation then you can just rephrase your request to ask for more money, opportunities or a clearer direction in what you are already doing.
I need an answer or a sign regarding this request in 48 hours. You can choose a longer time period for your answer, but don't make the time period for the response longer than a week. You wait to establish a habit of expecting the All that Is to communicate with you quickly, believe me it happens.

2. Allow the process to unfold.

In this step you will in a state of observation. Take a few minutes daily to sit in silence and contemplate something you always wanted to do, but never started. Or you could imagine yourself doing more of what you are already doing. It could be writing an article, starting a lawn care service, tutoring children, or learning to play a musical instrument.

3. Give Thanks

None of these new ideas might bring you immediate money but you are now opening yourself to the process and opening yourself to meet new people that will help in connecting to your purpose. Since I believe that we are all connected, rich, poor, young, old, black, white, hispanic and asian, then we have unlimited access to information and wealth. Sometimes that information or wealth is not our physically ours but because we can connect and make new friends and business contacts, the unlimited abundance of the universe is always available to us.

Appendix D

SETTING YOUR EMOTIONAL INTENTION

In this exercise you will be choosing an emotional vibration that may be higher than where you presently are emotionally. However, you are going to use the energy of the higher emotion to direct the energy by behind your daily activities.

Find an emotion on the chart that corresponds to what energy you would like to experience. Sit down and write about your feeling.

For this exercise I will use passion as an example:

As an exercise it might look like this.

I am passionate about my work.

I am enthused about the opportunities that are presented to me.

I attract what I project and because of this principle I am enthusiastic and passionate about creating new opportunities.

I expect more and more good to come to me because I feel excited about tomorrow.

Remember the Theory of the Quantum of Change. There is no time in reality that is without change. Whatever you focus on, wherever your attention is, that's where you emotional will go.

As you start to contemplate a more positive emotion, you will see that your breathing, your thoughts and then your emotions will start to slowly and sometimes very quickly embrace this new state. In the intention exercise you are using it to inspire you energetically for a short time period.

In Closing

Last summer in the US, as I begin this process I needed summer work, I had a few musical gigs not many but I was hopeful. I didn't have this process quite yet, but I did pray and meditate regularly. I was playing in a church for meal money and hanging out at the local Starbucks almost every day. I was meeting new people constantly. I really have always had a strong desire to teach and I taught publicly as a music teacher and later as a computer technology instructor.

Though a mutual friend I met the owner of a music school in Richmond, the Richmond Youth Jazz Orchestra, which is a subsidiary of Muse. The owner and I immediately hit it off. He invited me to the school to perform for the students and he hired me on the spot.

As you become more comfortable in letting the force guide your affairs you will find that there seems to be an infinitely intelligent spiritual presence working to your benefit.

Give Thanks and Expectation

The "Giving Thanks" step is my favorite step, because I never know exactly how my request is going to be answered. I never tire of the surprises. Over time I have gotten more confident with the QFIP, The Quantum of Change and the process of changing my emotional vibration. I expect something good to happen regularly and I accept the process. I have no doubt that the time delay is due to my own resistance or my own impatience with the process.

Oh, don't get me wrong, I still make phone calls, write songs, practice various instruments and look for new contacts. But I know that because I have put a request out into the Universe, I am already attracting what I need. Even if it might take longer than

I expected.

What happens when no answer appears or the request is not granted? In quantum physics there are two final principles I wish to share.

Effect 1 The Quantum Spin

The first one is the Quantum spin. Every thought, every desire, every piece of matter at some point is moving, spinning. Some matter or energies are moving at faster speeds than others, for example light and thought are actually vibrating faster than solid matter.

So sometimes to accelerate your request in being answered, you will have to increase your spin. You will have to look for interesting books to read, you will have to move out of your comfort zone and be willing to meet new people, visit new places, even explore moving to another city or country as I have. (This is in addition to the emotional work and reprogramming I've discussed throughout the book.)

Getting Unstuck

Whenever I get stuck I often like to go back and reread texts on Quantum Physics or authors like Pam Grout, the Hicks and Greg Kuhn. They always give me inspiration. I also look for new material that may give me new insights into what I am doing at present, be it music, business, gestalt psychology or quantum theory.

I regularly listen to inspirational podcasts, watch funny videos, or journal about what I am doing.

Effect 2 Antimatter – Anti-thoughts

In quantum physics when a set of quantum particles start to spin be it fermions, electrons or photons, there is another particle that appears out of nowhere from time to time, and it is called antimatter. This antimatter shows up randomly. If I compare the antimatter particle to quantum metaphysics in this context, the antimatter could be described as whatever inner thoughts of resistance to change that may be hidden within our belief system. Sometimes these anti-thoughts show up randomly, but trust me they will show up. Sometimes the resistance will be obvious and sometimes it will be hidden! Remember, partner up if you can!

Many of the desires of the heart will require us to examine our beliefs about what we think is possible and opening ourselves to the infinite nature of our reality.

Remember that you are reprogramming your subconscious mind, so repetition in many forms will quite often be necessary to create the new neural pathways that will undoubtedly lead to your success.

Often you may need to read this material over and over, listening to the audio version, until it becomes a part of your subconscious. I believe that whenever there is a lack then the anti-thought, that negative neural programming of past experiences, lack of spin, or some lack of energetic movement has occurred and the solution to that problem is me reconnecting with my beliefs about what I am trying to do.

LETTING GO

Sometimes I have a request that I may have to let go for the time being, as possibly I have more inner and outer work to do. Sometimes although I may be ready, there may be outer conditions that may need to change first. Outer conditions that I may not be aware of, but that the Source or QFIP is bringing into alignment if I am patient enough to wait through the process.
Einstein formulated his Theory of Relativity way before he was able

to prove to the world what he believed.

He had to wait almost a year before the planetary and solar conditions were in place to start the scientific experiment necessary to prove his hypothesis.

<u>Stay with the process. Move onto the next request; make notes about the present request. Keep reading about your request in your journal. Ask for clarity.</u>

Are there any preconditions? Are there preconditions about the request you need to have in place before the request can be honored? If so you may need to make a set of requests that deal with resolving the preconditions.

Quite often you may have to not only raise your emotional vibration, but you may have to contemplate the unlimited nature of the Quantum Field.

Time and again when receiving the informational aspect about a request, the information comes to me as a hunch or sometimes as an external event, like me meeting someone on the street or online by what appears to be a chance encounter. These synchronistic events are really quite obvious to me later.

Remember your emotions are psychic indicators of your reality. As you develop a greater mastery over this process you will naturally become more intuitive and psychically sensitive.

Why? Because your consciousness is like a quantum computer. It can do three incredible well and very quickly; 1) process previous information or experiences, 2) process current information and 3) make predictions about your future based on this information.

Now you have some new tools. 1) The QFIP, 2) Emotional Reference Chart, 3) Intending, and 4) The Request. You can now begin to change your present and future by examining what new ideas and new beliefs you need to acquire to improve your emotional state and be the Best You. For this is how you will attract the happiness and abundance you deserve. By understanding how to rewire your unconscious belief system and by repeatedly reading and listening to these principles they will start to take hold unconsciously. You will then have created the neural pathways of success you need to rewrite the current unconscious programming.

MEDITATION

The meditational aspect of these principles is important. Sometimes it is a good idea to reread your request. While doing so, you are going to sit quietly and pay attention to your breath.

Read your request, possibly a couple of times; imagine in your mind what it would like to have it answered. What it would feel like if your request was answered? Then continue focusing on your breathing. Don't be anxious, if your mind wanders, continue to breathe. Add a smile and a feeling of gratitude to your meditation. I often smile in meditation, for modern medicine has show that smiling releases a set of chemicals that increases your physical, mental and emotional well being.

I also smile because quite often I will immediately start to get ideas and information about my request when meditating.

I often remind myself about the many answers and resolutions to problems I have already received. This thought encourages me and reinforces this new set of beliefs. Well, that's it. You now have a new set of tools to begin to create the life you want. Remember whatever you are supposed to give the world only you can give the world in your unique way.

My personal coach use to tell me when I seemed to be going along badly on a project or struggling with a new emotional concept,

"Anything worth doing is worth doing badly."

Well I rephrase that quote here and say "Anything worth doing is worth doing as the BEST YOU, The Happiest You.

Enjoy.

Bibliography

Grout, Pam. E-Squared: Nine Do It Yourself Experiments That Prove Your Thoughts Create Your Reality. Hay House Press, 2013

Kuhn, Greg. How Physicists Build New Beliefs. Kindle Direct Publishing Edition, 2013

Hicks, Esther. Hicks, Jerry. Ask and It is Given. 2007

Schiller, Christoph. The Adventure of Physics: Quantum of Change. Motionmountain.net, 2012

Isaacson, Walter. Einstein: His Life and Universe. Simon & Schuster, 2007

About the Author

Warren Atiba Taylor is the author of 3 books. He has performed on and recorded 10 cds. Warren has toured and played festivals as a singer and saxophonist in over 10 countries. Formerly ordained as Tibetan Buddhist Monk, he had the opportunity to practice meditation with his holiness the Dalai Lama in 1987. He has taught meditation at several Unity Churches in the Washington, DC metropolitan area. He has written articles for jazz magazines and blogs in the US and Brazil.

Find out more about Warren at:
therevealingway.blogspot.com

Find out more info soon on the new website:
www.quantumsecrets.net

Available for coaching and lectures:
Contact: realatiba@gmail.com

Printed in Great Britain
by Amazon